Tadpole Books are published by Jump!, 5357 Penn Avenue South, Minneapolis, MN 55419, www.jumplibrary.com

Copyright ©2024 Jump. International copyright reserved in all countries. No part of this book may be reproduced in any form without written permission from the publisher.

**Editor:** Jenna Gleisner  **Designer:** Emma Almgren-Bersie  **Translator:** Annette Granat

**Photo Credits:** GlobalP/iStock, cover; Eric Isselee/Shutterstock, 1, 2bl, 4-5; clkraus/Shutterstock, 2tl, 2mr, 3, 6-7; Ninel Roshchina/Alamy, 2tr, 10-11; Donyanedomam/Dreamstime, 2ml, 12-13; Hung Chung Chih/Shutterstock, 2br, 8-9; Lee Yiu Tung/Shutterstock, 14-15; sanjagrujic/Shutterstock, 16tl; Menno Schaefer/Shutterstock, 16tr; FloridaStock/Shutterstock, 16bl; Rita_Kochmarjova/Shutterstock, 16br.

Library of Congress Cataloging-in-Publication Data
Names: Deniston, Natalie, author.
Title: Los pandas / por Natalie Deniston.
Other titles: Pandas. Spanish
Description: Minneapolis, MN: Jump!, Inc., (2024)
Series: Mis primeros libros de animales | Includes index.
Audience: Ages 3-6
Identifiers: LCCN 2023000288 (print)
LCCN 2023000289 (ebook)
ISBN 9798885248747 (hardcover)
ISBN 9798885248754 (paperback)
ISBN 9798885248761 (ebook)
Subjects: LCSH: Pandas—Juvenile literature.
Classification: LCC QL737.C27 D46518 2023 (print)
LCC QL737.C27 (ebook)
DDC 599.789—dc23/eng/20230117
LC record available at https://lccn.loc.gov/2023000288
LC ebook record available at https://lccn.loc.gov/2023000289

MIS PRIMEROS LIBROS DE ANIMALES

# LOS PANDAS

por Natalie Deniston

## TABLA DE CONTENIDO

**Palabras a saber**......................2

**Los pandas**...........................3

**¡Repasemos!**........................16

**Índice**...............................16

# PALABRAS A SABER

**bosque**

**come**

**juega**

**patas**

**pelaje**

**se trepa**

# LOS PANDAS

Un panda está en un bosque.

Él tiene un pelaje.

Él tiene patas.

**Él se trepa.**

Él come.

Él juega.

Él duerme.

# ¡REPASEMOS!

Los pandas son osos. ¿Puedes apuntar hacia otros osos abajo?

# ÍNDICE

bosque 3
come 11
duerme 15
juega 13

patas 7
pelaje 5
se trepa 9